How can Christians belie[ve]
[...] sleeps? Aren't you asham[ed]
[...] and magazines tell Musli[ms]
[...] god. Some Muslims there
[...] about this issue. Others, h[ave]
with an open mind. If that [is ... of you], then to you I direct this
interview. I would encourage you to read all of it before forming your
own conclusion.

1. Where did Christians get the idea that Jesus is the Son of God?

It is not a random idea that someone thought up. It is what the Word
of God says. It may surprise you to find out that Christians are
offended by the suggestion that Jesus is the *physical* son of God.
Perhaps you have been told that the term *Son of God* means that
Jesus was God's Son as a result of a physical relationship between
God and Mary. To Christians, however, such an idea is repugnant
and blasphemous. The Bible states that Jesus' conception took
place through the power of God Himself, not through any human or
physical agency, as it was explained to Mary by the angel Gabriel,
"behold, you will conceive in your womb and bring forth a Son, and
shall call His name Jesus. He will be great, and will be called the
Son of the Highest (God)" (Injil, Luke 1:31-32). Thirty years later
Jesus said to a man, "'Do you believe in the Son of God?' He
answered and said, 'Who is He that I may believe in Him?' And

Jesus said to him, 'You have both seen Him and it is He who is talking with you'" (Injil, John 9:35-37).

2. What does 'the Son of God' really mean?

It appears that a misunderstanding of the nature of Jesus' sonship occurred due to the confusion of two different terms for the word *son*. In Arabic, the word *walad* means "a physical boy born as a result of the marriage of a man and a woman." Of course, if this term is applied to the conception and birth of Jesus, it gives a totally false impression. It should be obvious that the sovereign God would not have a physical relationship with a human being.

The Arabic word *ibn*, however, is the word used for son throughout the Arabic translation of the Bible in reference to Jesus' relationship with God. The term *Ibnou-Rab* (Son of God) indicates a strong spiritual relationship.

Let's think about how we use the word son (ابن). Once when I asked a friend where he was from, he replied, 'I am the son of Tunisia.' Did he mean that Tunisia had a wife who gave birth? Of course not! What he meant is that he is Tunisian and has Tunisian characteristics. So when the Bible says that Jesus is the Son of God, it means that He has the characteristics of God. Those who speak Arabic will understand the following sentence, فلان عربي ابن عرب , (this man is an Arab, the son of an Arab). We use the phrase to emphasize the man's Arabic origin. He *really* is an Arab. So when the Bible says that Jesus is the Son of God, it means that He *really is* God. We also say, فلان ابن عشر سنوات (this man is a son of 10 years). We mean that his age *equals* 10 years. The phrase Son of God therefore indicates that Jesus is *equal to* God.

You see, the name Son of God does *not* mean that God had a wife. It does *not* mean that God married Mary who gave birth to Jesus. That would truly be a blasphemy. The meaning is far deeper. The prophets Abraham, Isaac, Moses, David and Isaiah would have understood the true meaning of the phrase 'the Son of God.'

What did the prophets of the Old Testament say about the coming of Jesus Christ?

The unique birth of Jesus Christ, which was foretold by numerous prophets, is one of the greatest supernatural events recorded in the Bible. A prophet called Isaiah spoke of Jesus' birth 700 years beforehand, saying, "For unto us a Child is born (Jesus), unto us a *Son* is given; and the government will be upon His shoulder. And His name will be called Wonderful, Counselor, Mighty God, everlasting Father, Prince of Peace" (Isaiah 9:6). Isaiah says that the Child "will be born to *us*," thus affirming the humanity of Jesus. But he also writes, "a Son will be *given* to us." Jesus was born of a woman - He was born to us, but His birth was of divine origin - He was *given* to us.

Isaiah said that the Son who was to come would be called:

Wonderful. This word is generally used in Hebrew to refer to the miraculous work of God. A miracle is something that is beyond the scope of human ability. In other words, it is something only God can do.

Counselor. His every instruction is wonderful. His opinions are extraordinary. His recommendations are without a fault. His advice is phenomenal. He is the only one worth listening to. Jesus is the wisdom of God. The promised Son would do things that only God can do. Just in case we are in any doubt, Isaiah tells us that this is a word he attributes to God: "This comes from the Lord of hosts, who is wonderful in counsel and excellent in guidance" (Isaiah 28:29).

Mighty God. This refers to the divinity and power of the Child to be born. This Child is the one of whom the apostle John would say 780 years later, "In the beginning was the Word (Jesus), and the Word was with God, and *the Word was God*...And the Word became flesh and dwelt among us, and we beheld His glory, the glory as of the only begotten of the Father, full of grace and truth" (John 1:1,14).

Everlasting Father. This literally means "Father of eternity." The rule of the promised Messiah knows no end. His government is like that of a father. In Jesus we have a love that will not let us go. George Matheson, a devout Christian who lived between 1842 and 1906, wrote about this love in a hymn that Christians sing in many churches today:

O Love that will not let me go,
I rest my weary soul in Thee.
I give Thee back the life I owe,
That in Thine ocean depths its flow
May richer, fuller be.

Prince of Peace. Jesus is the exclusive owner of peace. He said, "Peace I leave with you, My peace I give to you; not as the world gives do I give to you" (Injil, John 14:27). The peace that Jesus gives is a peace between God and man. Jesus offers peace to men and women through faith in Him. Many people are trying to make peace, but it has already been done. God has not left it for us to do; all we have to do is to enter into it.

So, long before a baby cried in a manger in Bethlehem, the prophet said that this Child would be unique. A human Child, yes, but a Child who was also divine. If you asked any Jewish person before the birth of Jesus, 'who can be called the Son of God?,' he or she would reply, 'only someone who is divine - equal to God.' That is why, when Jesus claimed to be the Son of God, they accused Him of blasphemy and crucified Him.

3. But Jesus never calls Himself the Son of God in the Bible…

Many Muslim friends make this claim. But it is not true. Jesus called Himself the Son of God many times. Here are some passages which prove it. One day Jesus asked His disciples a question, "'Who do you say I am?' Simon Peter answered, 'You are the Christ, *the Son of the living God.*' Jesus answered and said to him, 'blessed are you Simon for flesh and blood have not revealed this to you, but my Father who is in heaven'" (Matthew 16:15-17). When Jesus was arrested, the religious people who hated Him asked, "'Are you then *the Son of God?*' To this Jesus replied, 'You are right in saying that'" (Luke 22:70). Immediately they accused Him of blasphemy and asked for His crucifixion.

In other places Jesus spoke of God as 'My Father,' making clear that He is the Son of God. He said, "My *Father* gives you true bread from heaven …All that the *Father* gives to Me will come to Me and the one who comes to Me I will by no means cast out …And this is the will of Him who sent Me, that everyone who sees the Son and believes in Him may have everlasting life, and I will raise him up at the last day" (John 6:32,37,40). Elsewhere, Jesus said to His disciples, "He who has seen Me has seen the Father…do you not believe that I am in the *Father* and the *Father* in Me?" (John 14:9-11).

Once, the Jews said to Jesus, "'If You are the Christ, tell us plainly.' 'I told you , and you do not believe…My Father and I are one,'" Jesus replied. Then the Jews picked up stones to stone Him. But Jesus said to them, "'Many good works I have shown you from My Father. For which of those works do you stone Me?' 'For good work we do not stone You, but for blasphemy, and because You, being a Man, make Yourself God,' the Jews replied. Jesus answered them, "Is it not written in your law, 'I said, you are gods?' If He called them gods, to whom the word of God came (and the Scriptures cannot be broken), do you say of Him (Jesus) whom the Father sanctified and sent into the world, 'You are blaspheming,' because I said, 'I am the Son of God'?" (Injil, John 10:22-36).

4. So who is this Jesus: a prophet or more than a prophet?

If Jesus asked you the question, 'Who do you say I am?', what would your answer be? Perhaps you would reply that He is a great teacher or a prophet. Jesus asked His disciples the same thing, "Who do men say that I, the Son of Man, am?" (Mathew 16:13). The disciples replied, "Some say John the Baptist, some Elijah, and others Jeremiah or one of the prophets" (Matthew 16:14). It seems that, like you, some people of that day saw Jesus as simply a teacher or a prophet. Then Jesus asked His disciples again, "but who do you say that I am?" (Matthew 16:15). To this the apostle Peter answered, "You are the Christ, the Son of the Living God" (Matthew 16:16). What he was saying, in effect, is, "the people say You are a prophet, but I say that You are more than that. You are the Son of God." Jesus' response to Peter is very significant: "Blessed are you, Simon Peter, for flesh and blood has not revealed this to you, but My Father who is in heaven" (Matthew 16:17).

Was Jesus a prophet? Certainly. Was he only a prophet? Certainly not. Peter declared Him to be more than just a prophet.

The Bible is full of clear indications that Jesus is both Man and God. Throughout His life on earth He demonstrated the eternal attributes and characteristics of God Himself. He revealed to us the very nature of God. He said and did things which only God could say and do. He has divine names. He is able to forgive sin and change lives. He declared His unity with God. He has infinite power and knowledge. He was just and righteous. He was the only person who ever lived without sinning. The Qur'an itself points toward the sinless nature of Jesus (Surah 19, Maryam, Mary:19). Remember the many miracles Jesus performed: He raised the dead and healed the lame, the blind, the deaf, the dumb and the lepers. He cast out demons. He walked on water, stilled the storm, multiplied a few pieces of bread and fish to feed multitudes, and rose from the dead. At last, while His followers watched, He ascended bodily to heaven. Whenever people worshiped Him, He never rebuked them or rejected such worship, but accepted it as perfectly right! These are all signs of His deity.[1]

The late C.S. Lewis, a famous professor of Oxford and Cambridge Universities in England, was an agnostic who denied the deity of Christ for years. But eventually, in intellectual honesty, he submitted to Jesus as his God and Saviour after studying the overwhelming evidence for His deity. He observed, "You must make your choice. Either this man (Jesus) was, and is, the Son of God: or else a madman or something worse. You can shut Him up for a fool, you can spit at

---

[1] If you want to know more about the deity of Jesus, read our booklet entitled 'Who is this Jesus: a prophet or more than a prophet?'

Him and kill Him as a demon; or you can fall at His feet and call Him Lord and God. But let us not come up with any patronizing nonsense about His being a great human teacher. He has not left that open to us. He did not intend to."[2]

5. But why did God come in the likeness of men?

Why did God have to become man? What was the point? This is a very important question. It is the heart of Christianity. To know the answer, we must go back to the beginning of creation. We need to grasp what happened in the Garden of Eden.

Adam and Eve were told that the day they sinned, they would surely die. They ignored God and sinned, not by mistake, but through deliberate disobedience. Their bodies were eventually put in the grave. But, in one sense, Adam and Eve actually died the very day they sinned against God. They died spiritually. At first they had walked with God in a loving relationship. But when they disobeyed, sin formed a barrier between them and their Creator. There was an infinite gap between them and God. We call this spiritual death. It is because Adam was already spiritually dead that he died physically several hundred years later.

As a result of what happened in the Garden of Eden, all of us are born with a huge gap between us and God. God is holy and we are

---

[2] Mere Christianity, New York: Macmillan, 1952, pp. 40-41.

sinful, so we are cut off from Him. "Your iniquities have separated you from your God, and your sins have hidden His face from you," (The Bible, Isaiah 59:2). By nature we are separated from God. It is our disobedience which separates us. The prophet David wrote, "Behold, I was brought forth in iniquity, and in sin my mother conceived me" (Zabur, Psalm 51:5). Likewise, Paul the apostle said, "For all have sinned and fall short of the glory of God" (Injil, Romans 3:23). Every man is sinful at heart; though someone may seem to be very holy outwardly, there remain sins of wrong motives, sins of the mind.

The prophet Isaiah asked the question, "How then can we be saved?" He says, "We are all like an unclean thing, and all our righteousnesses are like filthy rags...and our iniquities, like the wind, have taken us away" (Isaiah 64:6).

What is the solution? Is there any hope? Many people try to bridge the gap by their own efforts. Some think they can get to God by being good religious people. They hope that their good deeds will outweigh their bad deeds enough to get them into paradise. But they never succeed. No one is perfect. It is not even that their contribution 'nearly but not quiet' reaches God. The reality is that we all infinitely short of the requirements. We can never reach God's standard by our own efforts. No matter how righteous we try to be, we are condemned by James 2:10 (Injil): "For whoever shall keep the whole law and yet stumbles in one point, he is guilty of all." Our sins can never be forgiven by striving toward self-righteousness. The gap between us and God is still there.

The question remains; what is the solution?

Once, when I was sitting quietly, I saw a troop of ants marching up and down a wall. They were trying to carry a grain of wheat to the top. But without success. The grain of wheat was too heavy. The pull of gravity was greater than their efforts! I pitied them. I wondered how I could help those hopeless ants. If I had reached down with my hand, I might have squashed some of them by mistake. They would have run away in fear. I could not help them. The only way I could have helped them was by becoming an ant, while keeping my human strength! Only that way could I help without terrifying them.

We are a bit like those ants. We can never reach God by our own efforts and good works. The gravity of our sin is too great. It is stronger than our efforts. Sin weighs heavily on our shoulders. But God pitied us. To liberate us from the tyranny of sin, He came in our likeness. He came as a man, but lived without sin. That was the main difference between Him and us. Who can re-establish the broken relationship between God and man? Surely, the only one who can bridge the gap is One who is both God and man.

Can religion restore my relationship with God?

Absolutely not! Imagine that one day you go to a swimming pool and jump into the deep water. You find yourself in trouble. You are drowning! You are dying, but you cannot save yourself because you do not know how to swim. You are hopeless and helpless. You shout for help. Someone approaches and yells, 'Get yourself together and save yourself! Come on mate, do it yourself!' What a terrible thing to say to a drowning man! A second person arrives on the scene and actually jumps into the water. He starts swimming. He says, 'Look at me. Learn how to swim and do the same. Then you will save yourself'. How ridiculous! There is no time for you to learn. In fact, a drowning man is absolutely incapable of learning anything. Now a third person approaches. He dives into the pool. He grabs you and drags you out of the water. You might resist Him, but out of love He saves you from death. Now, which one of these three people would you love most? Surely the third one.

Religion is like the first two people. By nature we are drowning in our sin. We are in a mess because of our separation from God. Religion tells us, 'Save yourself. Do this and that. Don't do this or that and you will be saved.' Some religious leaders are seen as examples. Their followers are told that if they imitate their lifestyle, they will be saved. It is like the second person who jumped into the water.

So religion cannot save us. We are hopeless. The Bible says that we are incapable of saving ourselves. That is why we need someone to jump into the water of our life and get hold of us and save us from our sin. This is exactly what God has done. God says to us, 'I know your situation. I know that you are separated from

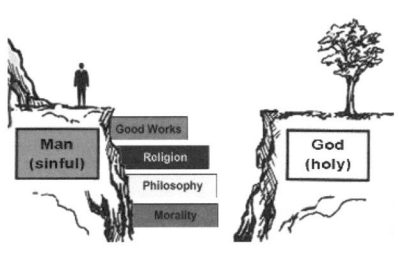

me. I know that your life is in a mess. I know that you cannot save yourself. And I know that giving you laws and commandments will not save you, because you can't and don't keep them. You are incapable of fulfilling them. But, I will come to where you are and get you out of the tyranny of your sin.' And so God came to this world in the Person of Jesus Christ. When someone allows Jesus to save him (by trusting in His death and resurrection), Jesus forgives his sin and grants him a place in paradise.

God has provided a way for sinners to be brought back to Him. "Christ also suffered once for sins, the just for the unjust, that He might bring us to God," (Injil, 1Peter 3:18). When Jesus died on the cross, He died as our perfect human substitute. He took the punishment that we deserve for our sin. He removed the barrier that separates us from God. But how could one man be the substitute for so many people? Since Jesus is also the divine Son of God, His sacrifice was enough to cover the sins of all those who believe in Him. To sin against the infinite God is to sin infinitely and therefore to

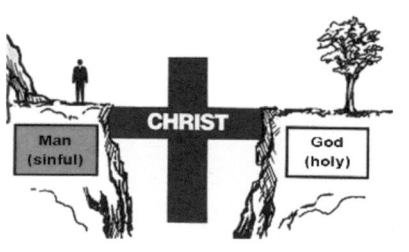

deserve infinite punishment. Left to ourselves we are lost. Only Jesus, the infinite Son of God, was able to take that infinite punishment in our place

6. Where does the Word of God say that Jesus is God in human form?

Jesus was different from every other man, in that He was God in the flesh. There are many verses in the Word of God that state this fact. Here are three examples: In his first letter to Timothy, Paul wrote, "*God was manifested in the flesh*, seen by angels, preached among the Gentiles, believed on in the world, received in glory" (Injil, 1 Timothy 3:16). Writing to a Church in Colosse (in Modern Turkey), Paul wrote, "In Christ all the fullness of *the Deity lives in body form*" (Injil, Colossians 2:9). Again, writing to another church, Paul said, "Let this mind be in you which was also in Christ Jesus, who, being in the form of God, did not consider it robbery to be equal with God, but made Himself of no reputation, taking the form of a bondservant, and coming in the likeness of men" (Injil, Philippians 2:5-7).

John, one of Jesus' disciples, wrote this, "In the beginning was the Word, …and the Word was God …And *the Word became flesh* and dwelt among us" (John 1:1, 14).

Did God cease to be God when He came in the form of man?

No! When God spoke to Moses from the bush, did He stop being God? Of course not. God cannot be limited by anything. When God revealed Himself in the form of a man, He was not limited by that humanity. He continued to rule the universe. He continued to be what He always had been (God), but in Jesus, He also became what He had never previously been (man). Jesus Christ was not 50% God and 50% man. He was 100% God and 100% man. Fully God and fully man. The divine Person took upon Himself a human nature. We really can't understand the mystery of how this happened. But it is conceivable, certainly, that God has the power to add to Himself a human nature and do it in such a way as to unite two natures in one Person.

Here's an illustration to explain this: Imagine a brilliant light. Now imagine that the light is put inside a glass. Does the glass stop the light shining? No! In fact, as the light is reflected by the glass, it shines even more brightly. In a similar way, when God became man in the Person of Jesus Christ, the body did not stop Him being God. Jesus said, 'I am the light of the world.' God became what He had never previously been (man) but He continued to shine and to rule the universe. In this way, He revealed Himself to the world *more clearly*.

What is your answer to Jesus?

I hope this has helped you to understand what the Holy Word of God means by calling Jesus 'the Son of God.' I hope you now see that Christians do not blaspheme the Almighty God. I pray that God, who loves the world so much, will help you to see this issue very clearly. This is one of the central truths of the Christian faith, "that you may believe that Jesus is the Christ, the Son of God; and that believing you may have life in His name" (Injil, John 20:31).

God wants us to turn away from our sin and to seek His mercy and forgiveness. "Return to the Lord and He will have mercy…and to our God for He will abundantly pardon" (Isaiah 55:7). God wants to help you and set you free from the bondage of sin. His desire is that you will also be saved from its consequences. He invites you to enter His family. God's promise is this: "as many as received Him (Jesus), to them He gave the right to become children of God, to those who believe in His name" (Injil, John 1:12).

God was so concerned about our situation, that He came to earth, taking the form of a man, so that you may know Him personally and be reconciled to Him. Will you receive Him?

How can I receive Jesus as my Saviour?

You can receive Jesus into your life, now, by talking to Him sincerely in prayer. Open your heart to Him, acknowledge and confess your